COUNTRY · EXPLORERS

A Visit to

EGYPT

By Hermione Redshaw

BEARPORT
PUBLISHING

Minneapolis, Minnesota

Credits

All images are courtesy of Shutterstock.com, unless otherwise specified. With thanks to Getty Images, Thinkstock Photo, and iStockphoto.

Cover – Orhan Cam, AlexAnton. 2–3 – givaga. 4–5 – givaga, ixpert. 6–7 – QQ7, Prin Adulyatham. 8–9 – 360b, zevana. 10–11 – WitR, Stefano Rulli. 12–13 – Triff, Irina Kononova. 14–15 – aleks333, oneinchpunch. 16–17 – Youssef Zakaria, diy13. 18–19 – Merydolla, MidoSemsem. 20–21 –AlexAnton, givaga. 22–23 – Mr.Music, Mountains Hunter.

Library of Congress Cataloging-in-Publication Data is available at www.loc.gov or upon request from the publisher.

ISBN: 979-8-88509-970-7 (hardcover)
ISBN: 979-8-88822-149-5 (paperback)
ISBN: 979-8-88822-290-4 (ebook)

© 2024 BookLife Publishing
This edition is published by arrangement with BookLife Publishing.

For more information, write to Bearport Publishing, 5357 Penn Avenue South, Minneapolis, MN 55419.

CONTENTS

COUNTRY TO COUNTRY

Which country do you live in?

A country is an area of land marked by **borders**. The people in each country have their own rules and ways of living. They may speak different languages.

Each country around the world has its own interesting things to see and do. Let's take a trip to visit a country and learn more!

Have you ever visited another country?

TODAY'S TRIP IS TO
EGYPT!

ASIA

EUROPE

NORTH AMERICA

AFRICA

Egypt

SOUTH AMERICA

AUSTRALIA

Egypt is a country mostly in the **continent** of Africa. Part of it is in Asia, too.

FACT FILE

Capital city: Cairo
Main language: Arabic
Currency: Egyptian pound
Flag:

Currency is the type of money that is used in a country.

CAIRO

We'll start our trip in Cairo! It is a very old city. Many amazing things from Cairo's history can be found in the Egyptian Museum.

Although Cairo is old, it has many modern buildings. Let's go to the top of Cairo Tower. We'll get a great view of the city from there.

THE PYRAMIDS

The tallest pyramid is the Great Pyramid of Giza.

The Great Pyramid of Giza

Next, we'll go just outside Cairo to see some pyramids. Many of these structures were built about 4,000 years ago. Egyptian **pharaohs** were often buried inside pyramids.

Some people believe the most important pharaohs were buried in the biggest pyramids. The Great Pyramid of Giza was built for a pharaoh named Khufu.

ANCIENT EGYPT

Hieroglyphic writing

Ancient Egyptians created one of the first forms of writing. They used **hieroglyphs**, or pictures, to stand for words and letter sounds. Ancient Egyptians used it to write about all sorts of things. Today, this writing helps us learn about Egyptian history.

Ancient Egyptians believed each pharaoh was like a living god. When a pharaoh died, they were **mummified** and wrapped in cloths. Then, the mummy would be put into a **sarcophagus** (sahr-KOF-uh-guhs).

Sarcophagus

CULTURE

Much of Egyptian **culture** has changed since ancient times. Today, **religion** is still important in Egypt. Many Egyptians are Muslim. This means they follow the religion of Islam.

Being welcoming and honest is important in Egypt.

Egypt is an **Arab** country. It has a similar culture to other Arab countries but has its own **traditions**, too.

ART AND MUSIC

Egypt is home to lots of art. At the Cairo Opera House, we can listen to modern and traditional music.

Cairo Opera House

Architecture has been an important art throughout Egyptian history. Ancient Egyptians carved huge statues out of stone. Today, modern Egyptian architecture reflects the buildings from its ancient history.

The Bibliotheca Alexandrina was built to remember the lost ancient Library of Alexandria.

RAMADAN

There are big festivals in Egypt for a holiday called Ramadan. This is an important month for Muslims. Houses are often decorated with lanterns known as fanoos.

During Ramadan, most Muslims avoid eating and drinking from sunrise to sunset. After sunset, people stay up to celebrate and eat.

THE NILE RIVER

The Nile River is one of the longest rivers in the world. It is more than 4,100 miles (6,600 km) long. The water in the Nile helps Egypt's plants and food crops grow.

Today, the Nile is surrounded by many modern buildings. It is sometimes used for traveling. Let's take a boat ride along the Nile River!

BEFORE YOU GO

We can't forget to go to El Gouna Film Festival. There, we can watch a lot of movies. Many filmmakers get a chance to show off their talents.

Be careful of stray cats. In ancient Egypt, many people thought cats brought luck. Cats are still common in Egypt today. Some people say the cats of pharaohs may still walk the streets!

What have you learned about Egypt on this trip?

GLOSSARY

Arab having to do with people originally from the Middle East and who speak Arabic

architecture a style or art of building design

borders lines that show where one place ends and another begins

continent one of the world's seven large land masses

culture the ideas, customs, and way of life shared by a group of people

hieroglyphs symbols from the writing system used by ancient Egyptians

mummified dried out and preserved so a body will not decay

pharaohs rulers of ancient Egypt

religion a set of beliefs used to worship a god or gods

sarcophagus a stone coffin

traditions customs, beliefs, or ways of doing something that has stayed the same for many years

INDEX

24